Mochi Recipes

The Best of Japan Food Culture

By

Heston Brown

HESTON BROWN

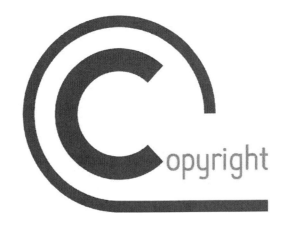

Copyright 2019 Heston Brown

Thank you so much for buying my book! I want to give you a special gift!

Receive a special gift as a thank you for buying my book. Now you will be able to benefit from free and discounted book offers that are sent directly to your inbox every week.

To subscribe simply fill in the box below with your details and start reaping the rewards! A new deal will arrive every day and reminders will be sent so you never miss out. Fill in the box below to subscribe and get started!

https://heston-brown.getresponsepages.com

Subscribe
to our
newsletter

Your Email

Table of Contents

Chapter I - Getting Started with Mochi!!

xxxxxxxxxxxxxxxxxxxxxxxxxxxxxxxxxxxxxxxxxxx

(1) Simple Mochiko

Mochiko ingredients provide you with enough carbohydrates required by the body along with delicious flavoured taste.

Total Prep Time: 10 minutes

Yield: 2

List of Ingredients:

- 2 cups Water
- 2 cups Mochiko
- 2 tablespoons Sugar

xxxxxxxxxxxxxxxxxxxxxxxxxxxxxxxxxxxxxxxxxxxx

Instructions:

1. Pour water into a pan.

2. Mix in Mochiko and sugar.

3. Let it cook for 6 minutes while you keep stirring.

4. Allow Mochiko to cool down after it has been cooked.

5. Make small balls out of it and add your desired filling to enjoy Mochi.

(2) Honey Mochi

You will be able to get enough fibre from the Honey Mochi dish so make sure to catch this recipe on your list!

Total Prep Time: 10 minutes

Yield: 2

List of Ingredients:

- 2 cups Rice flour
- 2 tablespoons Salt
- 2 tablespoons Sugar
- 2 cups Water
- 2 cups Adzuki beans
- 2 tablespoons Brown sugar
- 2 cups Water
- 2 tablespoons Honey

xxxxxxxxxxxxxxxxxxxxxxxxxxxxxxxxxxxxxxxxxx

Instructions:

1. Pour rice flour into a bowl.

2. Mix in salt, sugar, water and adzuki beans.

3. Add brown sugar and honey.

4. Add water while stirring it together.

5. Make small balls out of the dough and place them on the plate.

6. Heat them into the microwave for 3 minutes.

7. When ready, serve!

(3) Ice-Cream Mochi

Ice-cream Mochi recipe provides you with the energy which can last long for the whole day so do not miss out on this recipe!

Total Prep Time:10 minutes

Yield: 2

List of Ingredients:

- 2 cups Shiratamako
- 2 cups Water
- 2 tablespoons Sugar
- 2 tablespoons Corn starch
- 2 scoops Ice cream

Instructions:

1. Put shiratamako into a bowl.

2. Mix in water, sugar and corn starch.

3. Make small balls out of the mixture.

4. Heat it in the oven for 5 minutes.

5. When ready, let them cool down.

6. Now open the middle of the balls and add any flavoured ice-cream.

7. When done, serve!

(4) Potatoes Mochi

Potatoes never increase your weight but rather helps you put up with a healthy lifestyle, so make sure to learn this recipe!

Total Prep Time:10 minutes

Yield: 2

List of Ingredients:

- 3 Potatoes (boiled)
- 2 tablespoons Potato starch
- 2 cups Cheese
- 2 tablespoons Sweet potato powder
- 2 tablespoons Oil
- 2 tablespoons Sugar
- 2 tablespoons Soy sauce
- 2 cups Water

XXXXXXXXXXXXXXXXXXXXXXXXXXXXXXXXXXXXXXXXXX

Instructions:

1. Put potatoes into a bowl.

2. Add potato starch and mash the potatoes together.

3. Add cheese, potato powder, sugar and soy sauce.

4. Add water if the dough is too thick.

5. Make small balls out of the dough.

6. Heat the pan and add oil.

7. Place the balls in the pan and allow to cook on both sides for 10 minutes.

8. When ready, serve and enjoy!

(5) Coconut Milk Mochi

Amazing and delicious recipe made of rice flour which provides you with the proteins missing in your body!

Total Prep Time: 10 minutes

Yield: 2

List of Ingredients:

- 2 cups Rice flour
- 2 tablespoons Coconut milk
- 2 tablespoons Sugar
- 2 tablespoons Salt
- 2 cups Pindulus leaves

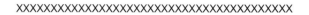

XXXXXXXXXXXXXXXXXXXXXXXXXXXXXXXXXXXXXXXXXX

Instructions:

1. Put rice flour into a bowl.

2. Mix in coconut milk, sugar, salt and Pindulus leaves.

3. Make sure there are no lumps in the batter.

4. Make small balls out of it and place them in a plate.

5. Heat the balls into the microwave for 4 minutes.

6. When ready, serve!

(6) Chicken Stock Mochi

Chicken stock works best for heart patients so learn this recipe now!

Total Prep Time: 10 minutes

Yield: 2

List of Ingredients:

- 2 Radish
- 1 Carrot
- 2 cups Soup stock
- 2 tablespoons Salt
- 1 tablespoon Ajinomoto
- 2 tablespoons Liquor
- 2 tablespoons Rice cake

xxxxxxxxxxxxxxxxxxxxxxxxxxxxxxxxxxxxxxxxx

Instructions:

1. Put radish into a pot.

2. Mix in carrot, soup stock, salt, ajinomoto and liquor.

3. Add rice cake.

4. Cook for 10 minutes.

5. When ready, serve!

(7) Dashi Mochi

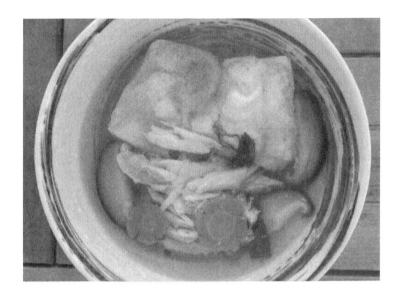

Mushrooms are good for the eyes and brain, so try this recipe now!

Total Prep Time: 10 minutes

Yield: 2

List of Ingredients:

- 2 cups Water
- 2 cups Dashi
- 2 tablespoons Mirin
- 2 cups Broccoli florets
- 2 cups Chicken tender
- 2 cups Mushrooms
- 2 cups Mochi blocks

xxxxxxxxxxxxxxxxxxxxxxxxxxxxxxxxxxxxxxxxx

Instructions:

1. Pour water into a bowl.

2. Mix in dashi and mirin.

3. Heat the pan and pour the mixture.

4. Cook for 4 minutes.

5. Mix in chicken tenders, mushrooms and Mochi blocks.

6. Cook for another 6 minutes on high heat.

7. When ready, serve!

(8) Bean Paste Mochi

Bean paste Mochi is the best source of zinc for the body so try this recipe for sure!

Total Prep Time: 10 minutes

Yield: 2

List of Ingredients:

- 2 cups Flour
- 2 cups Shiratamako
- 2 tablespoons Sugar
- 2 cups Water
- 2 tablespoons Food colour
- 2 tablespoons Bean paste
- 2 tablespoons Salad oil
- 2 cups Cherry blossoms leaves

xxxxxxxxxxxxxxxxxxxxxxxxxxxxxxxxxxxxxxxxx

Instructions:

1. Put flour into a bowl.

2. Mix in shiratamako, sugar, water, food colour and bean paste.

3. Stir gently.

4. Add salad oil into the bowl and pour the mixture into a saucepan.

5. Cook for 10 minutes.

6. When ready, make shapes out of it and wrap it around the cherry blossom leaves.

7. Enjoy the dish!

(9) Cute Sesame Mochi

A complete pack for you to get enough protein which can keep you healthy all the way!

Total Prep Time: 10 minutes

Yield: 2

List of Ingredients:

- 2 cups Mochi pieces
- 2 tablespoons Sugar
- 2 cups Nerikiri dough
- 2 tablespoons Food colour
- 2 tablespoons Black sesame

Instructions:

1. Put Mochi pieces into a bowl.

2. Mix in sugar, nerikiri dough, food colour and black sesame.

3. Heat the pan and make small balls out of the dough.

4. Cook them for 10 minutes.

5. When ready, mould it into any shape and serve.

(10) Ham and Cheese Nori Mochi

Looking forward to lose weight? Here is the best recipe for you to try tonight!

Total Prep Time: 10 minutes

Yield: 2

List of Ingredients:

- 2 cups Mochi rice cake
- 1 lb. Ham
- 2 tablespoons Cheese
- 2 pieces Nori
- 2 tablespoons Soy sauce
- 2 tablespoons Margarine

xxxxxxxxxxxxxxxxxxxxxxxxxxxxxxxxxxxxxxxxx

Instructions:

1. Put Mochi rice cake into a bowl.

2. Mix in ham pieces, cheese and soy sauce.

3. Melt margarine into a pan and add in the mixture.

4. Let it cook for 10 minutes.

5. Add nori.

6. Cook for another 2 minutes.

7. When ready, serve!

Chapter II - Mochi Dishes

xxxxxxxxxxxxxxxxxxxxxxxxxxxxxxxxxxxxxxxxx

(11) Kinako Mochi

A dish rich in vitamin A, C and E that keeps the body healthy and makes it function properly.

Total Prep Time: 10 minutes

Yield: 2

List of Ingredients:

- 2 cups Rice flour
- 2 cups Glutinous rice flour
- 2 tablespoons Warm water
- A pinch of Salt
- 2 cups Walnuts
- 2 cups Kinako
- 2 tablespoons Oil

XXXXXXXXXXXXXXXXXXXXXXXXXXXXXXXXXXXXXXXXXX

Instructions:

1. Pour rice flour into a bowl.

2. Mix in glutinous rice flour with warm water.

3. Make a dough out of it.

4. Add salt and kinako.

5. Pour oil into a pan and heat it slightly.

6. Place small portions of the mixture into the pan.

7. Cook for 10 minutes on both sides.

8. When ready, serve and enjoy with sprinkling walnuts.

(12) Tsubu-an Mochi

This recipe covers the deficiency of minerals in the body so make sure to learn this recipe to make the dinner delicious for your family today!

Total Prep Time: 10 minutes

Yield: 2

List of Ingredients:

- 2 cups Mochi
- 2 cups Rice–
- 2 cups Tsubu-an

Instructions:

1. Put Mochi pieces into a bowl and heat in the microwave for 2 minutes.

2. Add rice on top of it and mix well.

3. Place a palm full of mixture into your hand and then fill it with tsubu-an.

4. Cover from all sides and make small balls out of it.

5. Place them into the oven for 2 minutes.

6. When ready, serve and enjoy!

(13) Coconut flakes Mochi

Do not like to have coconut? They are one of the best sources to have enough carbohydrates for the body along with protein and you can find them both in this recipe.

Total Prep Time: 10 minutes

Yield: 2

List of Ingredients:

- 2 tablespoons Halaya
- 2 cups ko
- 2 cups Coconut flakes
- 2 tablespoons Butter
- 2 tablespoons White sugar
- 2 Eggs
- 2 cups Milk
- 2 tablespoons Baking powder
- 2 tablespoons Vanilla extract

xxxxxxxxxxxxxxxxxxxxxxxxxxxxxxxxxxxxxxxxxx

Instructions:

1. Pour halaya into a bowl.

2. Mix Mochiko, coconut flakes, butter and white sugar.

3. Add eggs, milk and baking powder.

4. Preheat oven to 350 F and pour the mixture into a baking tin.

5. Let it bake for 10 minutes.

6. In the middle of baking, add vanilla extract.

7. When ready, serve!

(14) Shiratamako potatoes Mochi

The healthy cod dish provides you more vitamins enrichment than being high in calories.

Total Prep Time:10 minutes

Yield: 2

List of Ingredients:

- 2 Potatoes (boiled)
- 2 tablespoons Sugar
- 1 tablespoon Salt
- 2 cups Shiratamako
- 1 tablespoon Kinako

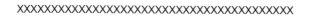

XXXXXXXXXXXXXXXXXXXXXXXXXXXXXXXXXXXXXXXX

Instructions:

1. Put potatoes into a pan and heat them lightly.

2. Mash them into a bowl.

3. Mix in sugar and salt.

4. Now make small balls out of the mixture and add shiratamako with kinako in the middle.

5. Place them into a plate and cover with a wrap.

6. Heat in the oven for 2 minutes.

7. When ready, serve and enjoy!

(15) Simple Baked Egg Filled Mochi

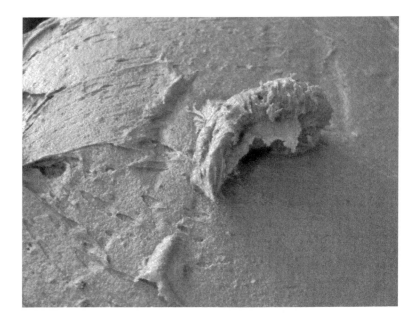

Eggs work best for vitamins and minerals coverage in your body!

Total Prep Time: 10 minutes

Yield: 2

List of Ingredients:

- 2 cups Rice flour
- 2 tablespoons Sugar
- 2 cups Coconut milk
- 2 cups Evaporated milk
- 2 tablespoons Baking powder
- 2 tablespoons Vanilla extract
- 2 Eggs
- 2 tablespoons Melted butter

xxxxxxxxxxxxxxxxxxxxxxxxxxxxxxxxxxxxxxxx

Instructions:

1. Pour rice flour into a bowl.

2. Mix in sugar, coconut milk, evaporated milk, baking powder and vanilla extract.

3. Grease the oven dish with butter.

4. Pour the mixture into the dish. Let it bake in the oven at 350 F for 10 minutes.

5. Now, whisk eggs and pour it in the middle of the baked bread.

6. Let it heat for 2 minutes.

7. When ready, serve and enjoy!

(16) Daikon Radish Mochi

Rice flour is beneficial for the eyes and the brain which is why it is healthy to have it at least once a week.

Total Prep Time:10 minutes

Yield: 2

List of Ingredients:

- 2 cups Daikon radish
- 1 tablespoon Salt
- 2 tablespoons Rice flour
- 2 cups Katakuriko
- 2 cups Chicken soup stock
- 2 cups Water
- 2 tablespoons Vegetable oil

XXXXXXXXXXXXXXXXXXXXXXXXXXXXXXXXXXXXXXXXXX

Instructions:

1. Pour water and salt into a pan.

2. Heat it slightly and then add rice flour. Stir gently.

3. Add katakuriko and chicken soup stock.

4. Mix with vegetable oil.

5. Cook for 10 minutes.

6. When ready, serve!

(17) Custard Mochi

Delicious yet amazing custard flavoured recipe.

Total Prep Time:2

Yield:

List of Ingredients:

- 2 cups Mochiko flour
- 2 tablespoons Baking powder
- 2 tablespoons Sugar
- 2 tablespoons Melted butter
- 2 Eggs
- 2 cups Coconut milk
- 2 tablespoons Vanilla
- 2 tablespoons Sesame seeds
- 2 cups Custard (cooked)

XXXXXXXXXXXXXXXXXXXXXXXXXXXXXXXXXXXXXXXX

Instructions:

1. Pour Mochiko flour into a bowl.

2. Mix in baking powder, sugar, butter and eggs.

3. Cook in a microwave oven for 2 minutes.

4. Add coconut milk, vanilla and sesame seeds.

5. Heat it in the microwave oven for 10 minutes.

6. When ready, make small shapes out of it and add custard in the middle.

7. Serve and enjoy!

(18) Okara Mochi

Okara Mochi tastes delicious and also covers up the lack of
nutrients retaining in your body from a long time.

Total Prep Time: 10 minutes

Yield: 2

List of Ingredients:

- 2 cups Fresh Okara
- 1 Banana
- 1 tablespoon Joshinko
- 2 tablespoons Sugar
- 2 cups Barley flour
- 2 tablespoons Cinnamon powder
- 2 tablespoons Powdered sugar

xxxxxxxxxxxxxxxxxxxxxxxxxxxxxxxxxxxxxxxxx

Instructions:

1. Pour okara into a bowl.

2. Mix mashed banana, joshinko, sugar and barley flour.

3. Add cinnamon powder and stir well.

4. Make small shapes out of the mixture in any shape.

5. Heat it in the microwave for 2 minutes.

6. When ready, sprinkle powdered sugar to serve!

(19) Chocolate Mochi Brownies

Try the chocolate Mochi for full flavoured Mochi recipe if you have never had it before.

Total Prep Time: 10 minutes

Yield: 2

List of Ingredients:

- 2 cups Mochi flour
- 2 tablespoons Sugar
- 2 tablespoons Cocoa powder
- 2 Eggs
- 2 cups Cream
- 2 cups Tofu
- 2 tablespoons Baking soda
- 2 tablespoons Chocolate chips powder

XXXXXXXXXXXXXXXXXXXXXXXXXXXXXXXXXXXXXXXXX

Instructions:

1. Pour Mochi flour into a bowl.

2. Mix in sugar, cocoa powder, eggs and cream.

3. Heat it in a microwave oven for 3 minutes.

4. Now add baking soda and chocolate chips powder.

5. Mix well and make small balls out of it.

6. Make sure the tofu is cooked and soft beforehand.

7. To serve, place tofu beside the Mochi balls and enjoy!

(20) Tapioca Mochi

One of the best dishes to cook if you are planning for a weight loss plan!

Total Prep Time: 10 minutes

Yield: 2

List of Ingredients:

- 2 cups Tapioca flour
- 2 cups Coconut milk
- 2 tablespoons Sugar
- 2 tablespoons Soy beans
- 2 tablespoons Muscovado syrup

xxxxxxxxxxxxxxxxxxxxxxxxxxxxxxxxxxxxxxxxx

Instructions:

1. Pour tapioca flour into a bowl.

2. Mix coconut milk, sugar, soy beans and muscovado syrup.

3. Stir gently.

4. Pour the mixture into a microwave oven dish and heat it for 4 minutes.

5. When ready, cut it in any shape to serve!

(21) Tri-Colour Mochi

The combination of these Mochi is amazing and it provides you with protein and is rich in Vitamin A as well.

Total Prep Time:10 minutes

Yield: 2

List of Ingredients:

- 2 tablespoons Mochiko
- 2 cups Sugar
- 2 tablespoons Baking powder
- 2 cups Coconut milk
- 2 cups Water
- 2 tablespoons Vanilla

XXXXXXXXXXXXXXXXXXXXXXXXXXXXXXXXXXXXXXXXX

Instructions:

1. Pour Mochiko into a bowl.

2. Mix in sugar, baking powder, coconut milk and water.

3. Stir well.

4. Add vanilla.

5. Heat the mixture in the oven for 10 minutes.

6. When ready, make small shapes out of it to enjoy!

Chapter III - Variety of Mochi Recipes

xxxxxxxxxxxxxxxxxxxxxxxxxxxxxxxxxxxxxxxxxx

(22) Yomogi Mochi

Mochi helps you to reduce weight and does not make you feel heavy on the stomach so make sure to try this recipe.

Total Prep Time: 10 minutes

Yield: 2

List of Ingredients:

- 2 cups Yomogi
- 2 tablespoons Tsubu-an
- 2 tablespoons Sugar
- 2 tablespoons Joshinko
- 2 tablespoons Shiratamako
- 2 cups Hot water
- 2 tablespoons Baking soda

xxxxxxxxxxxxxxxxxxxxxxxxxxxxxxxxxxxxxxxx

Instructions:

1. Boil the water and add baking soda.

2. Let it boil for 2 more minutes.

3. Add yomogi and rinse it.

4. Now add Tsubu-an and cook for 2 more minutes.

5. Add sugar, shiratamako and joshinko into the bowl.

6. Mix the Tsubu-an mixture.

7. Make small shapes out of it and chill in refrigerator.

8. When ready, serve.

(23) Simple Okara Mochi

You will love the taste and the associated nutrients will keep your brain fresh throughout the day.

Total Prep Time: 10 minutes

Yield: 2

List of Ingredients:

- 2 cups Fresh Okara
- 2 cups Katakuriko
- 3 cups Water

XXXXXXXXXXXXXXXXXXXXXXXXXXXXXXXXXXXXXXXXX

Instructions:

1. Pour fresh okara into a bowl.

2. Mix katakuriko and water. Gently combine all the ingredients until there are no lumps.

3. Now divide the mixture into eight sections. Cover it with a plastic wrap and microwave for 2 minutes.

4. Let it get bigger in size and then enjoy the delicious Mochi.

(24) Azuki Beans Mochi

Azuki beans works great for the liver and heart so try it with full of protein today!

Total Prep Time: 10 minutes

Yield: 2

List of Ingredients:

- 2 cups Water
- 2 tablespoons Caster sugar
- 2 tablespoons Matcha
- 3 cups Water
- 2 cups Shiratamako
- 2 tablespoons Hojicha
- 2 tablespoons Cocoa powder
- 2 tablespoons Azuki beans
- 2 cups Cornflakes

XXXXXXXXXXXXXXXXXXXXXXXXXXXXXXXXXXXXXXXX

Instructions:

1. Put hot water into a bowl.

2. Mix with sugar and heat it in the oven for 2 minutes.

3. Combine shiratamako with water into another bowl. Add cocoa powder and mix well.

4. Add hojicha powder, azuki beans, cornflakes and sugar.

5. Make small balls out of the mixture.

6. Heat it in the microwave for 2 minutes.

7. When ready, serve!

(25) Shiro Dashi Mochi

Once you start to have this recipe of Mochi, you will see how energetic and light you will feel in your stomach.

Total Prep Time: 10 minutes

Yield: 2

List of Ingredients:

- 2 cups Fresh Okara
- 2 Onion (chopped)
- 2 tablespoons Ginger (grated)
- 1 tablespoon Shiro dashi
- 2 tablespoons Katakuriko
- 2 tablespoons Soy sauce
- 2 tablespoons Olive oil

XXXXXXXXXXXXXXXXXXXXXXXXXXXXXXXXXXXXXXXXX

Instructions:

1. Pour okara into a bowl.

2. Mix shiro dashi and katakuriko. Stir gently.

3. Now make large balls out of it and then flatten the top with a spoon.

4. Pour oil into a frying pan and heat it lightly, Fry the balls you made.

5. Remove from pan and add onion with garlic in it.

6. Add soy sauce. Cook for 2 minutes.

7. Pour the mixture over the balls to enjoy Mochi!

(26) Takana Pickles Mochi

Pickles are a rich source of potassium and zinc for the body so do not miss out on this recipe!

Total Prep Time: 10 minutes

Yield: 2

List of Ingredients:

- 2 Potatoes (boiled)
- 2 cups Shiratamako
- 2 cups Water
- 1 tablespoon Salt
- 2 tablespoons Sesame oil
- 2 tablespoons Takana pickles
- 1 Chicken soboro

XXXXXXXXXXXXXXXXXXXXXXXXXXXXXXXXXXXXXXXXX

Instructions:

1. Take off the skin of potatoes and mash them into the bowl.

2. Add shiratamako and water. Mix well and make sure there are no lumps.

3. Split it into portions and make small round shapes.

4. Brush the balls with sesame oil and place them into a frying pan.

5. Heat them lightly and let them turn light brown.

6. Fill the Mochi with pickles and chicken.

7. When ready, serve and enjoy!

(27) Katakuriko Mochi

This Mochi recipe helps you in digestion and keeps the immune system strong and prevents stomach problems in the future.

Total Prep Time: 10 minutes

Yield: 2

List of Ingredients:

- 2 cups Fresh okara
- 2 cups Katakuriko
- 2 cups Water
- 1 pack Ochzuke mix

xxxxxxxxxxxxxxxxxxxxxxxxxxxxxxxxxxxxxxxxx

Instructions:

1. Pour okara into a bowl.

2. Mix in katakuriko and water. Stir gently.

3. Add ochzuke and let it settle for 2 minutes.

4. Make round shapes out of the mixture and heat the frying pan.

5. You do not need oil so put the balls into the pan and fry for 2 minutes on each side.

6. When ready, serve and enjoy!

(28) Mochi Rice

A soft and light diet for you to eat anytime you want, which digests quickly too so you do not have to worry even if you eat it at night time.

Total Prep Time: 10 minutes

Yield: 2

List of Ingredients:

- 2 cups Mochi rice
- 2 cups Water
- 2 tablespoons Sugar

Instructions:

1. Put water and Mochi rice into a blender.

2. Blend until it looks thick and heavy.

3. Pour it into a bowl and heat it in the microwave for 3 minutes.

4. Stir the mixture and then make small balls out of it.

5. Serve and enjoy!

(29) Okaramoti Mochi

A beautiful dish with unlimited nutrients which you would love to cook tonight.

Total Prep Time: 10 minutes

Yield: 2

List of Ingredients:

- 2 cups Fresh Okara
- 1 cup Katakuriko
- 2 cups Water
- 1 Adzuki beans (can)

XXXXXXXXXXXXXXXXXXXXXXXXXXXXXXXXXXXXXXXXXX

Instructions:

1. Pour okara into a bowl.

2. Mix katakuriko and water.

3. Now add adzuki beans and mash them together.

4. Make small shapes out of it and place it on a plate.

5. Wrap the plate and heat it in a microwave for 3 minutes.

6. When ready, serve and enjoy!

(30) Strawberry Filled Mochi

Strawberries are one of the best sources of fibre and vitamins to the body and keep you in shape also.

Total Prep Time: 10 minutes

Yield: 2

List of Ingredients:

- 2 cups Strawberries
- 2 tablespoons Shiratamako
- 2 tablespoons Cocoa powder
- 2 tablespoons Strawberry powder
- 2 cups White chocolate
- 2 tablespoons Heavy cream
- 2 tablespoons Sugar
- 2 cups Water

XXXXXXXXXXXXXXXXXXXXXXXXXXXXXXXXXXXXXXXXX

Instructions:

1. Cut the strawberries into a heart shape and keep it aside.

2. Add cream into a bowl while adding white chocolate.

3. Heat it in a microwave for 2 minutes and add cream in it.

4. Make the mixture into small balls and place strawberries on its top.

5. Place into the fridge to chill.

6. Now add shiratamako separately into a bowl.

7. Mix sugar, strawberry powder, cocoa powder and water.

8. Heat in a microwave for 2 minutes.

9. When ready, take the strawberries out of the fridge and cover them with this mixture.

10. Serve and enjoy!

About the Author

Heston Brown is an accomplished chef and successful e-book author from Palo Alto California. After studying cooking at The New England Culinary Institute, Heston stopped briefly in Chicago where he was offered head chef at some of the city's most prestigious restaurants. Brown decide that he missed the rolling hills and sunny weather of California and moved back to his home state to open up his own catering company and give private cooking classes.

Heston lives in California with his beautiful wife of 18 years and his two daughters who also have aspirations to follow in their father's footsteps and pursue careers in the culinary arts. Brown is well known for his delicious fish and chicken dishes and teaches these recipes as well as many others to his students.

When Heston gave up his successful chef position in Chicago and moved back to California, a friend suggested he use the internet to share his recipes with the world and so he did! To date, Heston Brown has written over 1000 e-books that contain recipes, cooking tips, business strategies for catering companies and a self-help book he wrote from personal experience.

He claims his wife has been his inspiration throughout many of his endeavours and continues to be his partner in business as well as life. His greatest joy is having all three women in his life in the kitchen with him cooking their favourite meal while his favourite jazz music plays in the background.

Author's Afterthoughts

Thank you to all the readers who invested time and money into my book! I cherish every one of you and hope you took the same pleasure in reading it as I did in writing it.

Out of all of the books out there, you chose mine and for that I am truly grateful. It makes the effort worth it when I know my readers are enjoying my work from beginning to end.

Please take a few minutes to write an Amazon review so that others can benefit from your opinions and insight. Your review will help countless other readers make an informed choice

Thank you so much,

Heston Brown

Made in the USA
Lexington, KY
19 June 2019